Dear Larry, Gill
& Chloé,
Hope this will be a reminder
of your time in the Caribbean!
We will miss you!
Much love
Matt & Jodie
+ Emily

Dear Larry & Gill
& Chloé
Wishing you all the
very best & I will
miss you. Good Luck
from Sue & Graham.

Dear Gill & Larry & Chloe,
We wish you all the very best
for the future. Hope to meet
up wherever!!
All our love
Selina, Walter, Molly
+ Finlay xx

Dear Gill & Larry & Chloe,
All our very best for your
new life in your new destination.
We will surely miss you.
Keep in touch.
Joe & Lucy + kids.

Dear Jill & Larry,
Best wishes,
where-ever your travels
take you! We
will miss you.
Adrian & Patti

Dear Larry & Gill,
We all wish you the
very best in your new
venture / we are really
going to miss you & hope
we'll meet up again
somewhere / somehow.
Lots of love
Richard, Hayden,
Oliver & Isabelle

Dear Jill & Larry,
With very best wishes
as you move on from TTT
It was wonderful knowing
you all.
Love Roger + Nicki.

To Chloé!
Oliver is going to miss
you sooooo much - you've
been friends since you
were 1 yr old & he's
not looking forward to his
life here in TTT
without you.
Love
Rebecca, Woodrow &
Oliver

Dearest Jill & Larry,
Enjoyed building a
friendship with the two
of you and looking forward
to future endeavors &
around the world.
Looking forward to visits
...... Dave & Tino Spik

Good Luck Gill, Larry &
Chloé.
You know, I'm really going
to miss seeing your
black spotty balls every
week Larry!
love Jim, Lou, Ryan

MACO

CARIBBEAN HOMES

TOUTE BAGAI PUBLISHING LIMITED

To Scipio and Sandy who taught me to
acknowledge and savour the beauty of our islands

[signature]

Toute Bagai Publishing Ltd
101 Tragarete Rd,
Woodbrook, Port of Spain
Trinidad, West Indies

Email: distribution@macomag.com

www.macomag.com

ISBN: 978 976 8194642

First Published in 2005

Designed by Marie France Aqui of U&I Design Studio Limited
Cover design by Marie France Aqui of U&I Design Studio Limited
Cover photograph by Mike Toy

Printed and bound in China

TABLE OF CONTENTS

INTRODUCTION

Light. Air. Colour.

This trinity of blessings may be regarded as the primary asset of life in the Caribbean. The way the sunshine illuminates the water, like sequins scattered across fine silk; the morning mist rising like an angel's breath from the indigo mountains; the expanse of the blue heavens with rolling white cloud; even the sudden thunderous grey whipping skies all have a dramatic beauty.

The advantages of our climate, as much as our robust historical background, greatly influence the way we live. Ever since Columbus sailed to the New World in the 15th century, the world has been coming to our doorsteps—some by choice, others because they were obligated to. Our history has been turbulent but an amazing blend of cultures has also been created in small places, enlarging our horizons before we ever set sail or board a plane to faraway cities and towns.

Our islands have been squabbled over and ruled by the French, Spanish, Dutch, English. Millions of Africans were transported here in the holds of slave ships to work the sugar-cane fields and after their freedom had been grudgingly declared, a number of experiments was conducted to find suitable labour replacements, bringing the Indians, Chinese and Portuguese to these shores.

The old explorers and conquerors never found their city of El Dorado but can any price be placed upon the wealth of the region? Nowhere else can such a mixture of elements, memories and influences be found in such a small scattering of territories. Our islands may be tiny, some flat, some rocky, some lying there like rumpled emerald silk encircled in blue. Some are coral dry, others are drenched by rains for months and months. But aaah, there is the light, the air, the colour.

Climate and history—we all must bow to these two powerful elements. These forces have helped mold us into a region of people known for their vibrancy, creativity and sheer love of life, qualities which are reflected in the houses and interiors we create.

In 1999, MACO Caribbean Living magazine was born and since then has showcased numerous unique homes throughout the Caribbean. The time came to create a keepsake, a memoir of some of our old favourites, as well as some new ones, found along the way. MACO Caribbean Homes is a collection of 16 dwellings in 12 islands, each distinctive, each with a different mood, reflecting the personalities of the owners. From a stately and imposing restored plantation house in Antigua to a Trinidad gingerbread house, painted in Carnival colours, to an African-influenced abode in Carriacou, the collection illustrates the rich blend of influences characteristic to the Caribbean.

While the collection is not meant to be an architectural text, it nevertheless illustrates a variety of architectural styles, some traditional West Indian, as seen in demerara windows, gingerbread fretwork, galleries and verandas, while others reflect the influence of external aesthetics. Whether the owners are born West Indians or travellers who have chosen to live here, they have embraced light, air, colour.

From an opulent Asian compound in Mustique to a nest on the face of a cliff in St Lucia, these houses were created for outdoor living, as displayed by the wraparound verandas, galleries, loggias, terraces, courtyards, gazebos, outdoor showers, and huge arches framing mountain and sky and sea and sand. Even a peculiar Hobbit-like underground retreat in Grenada offers a breezy, panoramic view of the Caribbean Sea from the dramatic open deck of its spacious veranda. And the gardens—tumbling bougainvillea, majestic palms, lotus ponds and sprawling tamarinds. The houses all have gardens like Eden.

The rich variety of building materials available in the region——Barbados coral stone; pink, grey and fawn volcanic rock in St Lucia, Carriacou stone; Guyanese wallaba and purpleheart wood—has been drawn upon by the architects and builders, adding colour, texture and character.

This book is a tribute to the confidence, creativity and imagination of the people who created these living spaces. Hopefully, it also provides a pause in the whirl of modern living, an opportunity to celebrate the best of ourselves, to stop, smile, take note and applaud.

Light. Air. Colour. This, too, is Caribbean living. Celebrate.

AT HOME WITH HISTORY

ANTIGUA

*An Antiguan plantation house survives hurricane damage
to re-emerge with new symmetry and majestic beauty*

Adapted from original article by **Diana Loxley**   Photography by **Julie Webster**

Nestled at the bottom of Fig Tree Drive, Antigua's rain forest, lies Body Pond estate house. Legend has it that it is so named because slaves used to hurl themselves to death in the waters below.

The 700-acre estate was built in 1682 by Governor Stapleton of the Leeward Islands. Stapleton's brother, Redmond, was the first owner. In 1801, he sold it to James Athill, Speaker of the House of Assembly. The house later passed through several owners, including Steve and Carrie Crotty, who laid the groundwork for the magnificent tropical garden. The present owners are Rob Sherman, a hotelier, and his wife Bernadette, who runs three restaurants and a trading company.

"When we moved here, the house was quite small and simple, very basic, with no upper floors, just lower and main floor levels," says Bernadette. The property, which is now scaled down to three acres, would originally have comprised the main living area, the paymaster's room, the great room and one bedroom.

Antiguan plantation houses used to be simple structures with a minimum of detailing, unlike the grander estate houses found in Jamaica and Barbados, where English architectural styles were transplanted with only minor modifications. "The house is a perfect example of that," says architect Mitch Stuart.

The Shermans wanted the house to be a place where their two children could grow up comfortably and so, they created a warm and relaxed ambiance. Bernadette Sherman, relying on her own flair and imagination, created different moods in each area. With a dramatic display of colour (raspberry with blue, yellow with pink) the house flows from classic grandeur to eclectic contemporary.

The Shermans also stripped out dark wood floors and replaced them with a lighter soft wood. The original stone walls, some two and a half feet thick, were built from ship's ballast, which was used to balance the empty merchant ships on their outward passage from England. The interior is of brick and rubble and the Shermans left the brickwork exposed in some areas to bring texture and warmth to the interior.

The original main entrance, an imposing octagonal room, remains untouched. In plantation days, this area functioned as the paymaster's room, where workers would collect their meagre wages. This room leads on to a spacious magnificent dining area, the centrepiece of the house.

The house now comprises six bedrooms and five bathrooms. A pool and a guest bedroom above the two-car garage were also added but the most substantial phase of renovation was undertaken between 1999 and 2000, following considerable hurricane damage.

A third storey was added and the master bedroom was relocated to the new level, taking full advantage of the breeze and magnificent views. The grand master suite includes a dressing room, glorious marble bathroom with a free-standing bath and a shower open to the sky. Exposed joints, timber planking, pitched roofs, pine floors and louvred windows on the upper level lend an airiness and definition to the interior. The original master bedroom is now a family room and access to the upper floor was created by a magnificent mahogany staircase.

Perhaps the most dramatic change is the addition to the rear of the house of an outside staircase leading down from the main veranda to the pool area. "Here," says Stuart, "we were aiming to introduce symmetry to the exterior of the house and this was achieved by the construction of a double staircase." The grandeur of the staircase is enhanced by the majestic royal palms behind the pool.

Bernadette Sherman calls the house her oasis but also sees herself as a caretaker for a piece of Antiguan history. "This is a historic house," she says, "and we are so fortunate to be passing through it."

The property's original stone walls, some two and a half feet thick, were built from ship's ballast, used to balance merchant ships on their outward passage from England. The interior of the house is brick and rubble and instead of plastering it over, the Shermans left the brickwork exposed to bring texture and warmth to the home. The books are a natural part of the ambiance. Bernadette Sherman has degrees in psychology and education from the University of Beirut and established a school in Antigua, called Island Academy.

Relying on her own flair, Bernadette Sherman re-shaped a 17th century plantation house into an oasis for her family on Body Pond Estate, Antigua. Although the house is ancient, she wanted her home to be inviting and comfortable for her children, as reflected by her colourful and cosy dining table.

Left: Skillful use of vibrant colour introduces warmth, drama and vitality to the downstairs hallway.

Far left: With its contrasting textures and forms, this magnificent kitchen translates traditional Caribbean architectural features into a modern context. The original stonework, high-pitched roof and stripped timber flooring lend character and airiness to the interior.

Instead of sleek, modern style, this bathroom remains true to the spirit of the house, with the exposed stone, wood ceiling and unobtrusive fittings and accessories. Yet, it is designed on a grand, luxurious scale-an indoor bathroom with an outdoor ambiance.

17

Left: A large copper, once used in the sugar industry, becomes a lily pond, bringing the old world into the new. Body Pond Estate, built in 1682, was once a thriving sugar cane plantation. It takes its name from the island's only river, where, it is said, slaves used to hurl themselves into the water to a tragic death.

Right: Perhaps, the most dramatic renovation is the double flight of stairs leading from the main veranda to the swimming pool. Previously, to get to the pool, one had to use an interior stairway, from the main terrace to the lower level bedroom, an unsightly, intrusive feature, which took up a substantial portion of the terrace. The grandeur of the staircase is enhanced by the majestic royal palms behind the pool.

ESCAPE TO SMUGGLER'S NEST

ST LUCIA

Privacy is the most precious asset at St Lucian hideaway
with commanding views of the ocean, mountains and sky

Adapted from original article by **Victor Marquis**   Photography by **Julie Webster**

There it was—perched on the cliff top on the Cap Estate shoreline, with commanding views of the blue Caribbean Sea and the neighbouring island of Martinque.

The house at Smuggler's Cove, just north of the seaside town of Gros Islet, St Lucia, was not visible from the road. It took a hike along concrete steps cut into an almost perpendicular cliff face leading down to the beach to stumble upon Smuggler's Nest.

The starkness of the almost blinding white walls is relieved by dark wood trim. The house has an abundance of terraces, patios and restful lounging areas scattered around the house. One gazebo overlooks the sea and the other is tucked away in the garden.

The two-and-a-half acre property is landscaped with a network of footpaths, which make for long, leisurely strolls among the greenery. There is a large, irregularly-shaped swimming pool, which also affords a great view of the ocean. The pool's asymmetrical shape, the black tiles which ring it and the giant trees overshadowing it give the impression that one is in a grotto, carved out by Nature.

The house is built on three levels, with alcoves here and there and balconies that flow from one room to the other. The open-plan design takes advantage of the cooling breezes while embracing the views of the ocean and the northern coastline (Pigeon Island with its connecting causeway and historical military ruins lies just below and to the left from wherever you look.)

Designed by Ian Morrison, the house was built by Marc Johnson, a building contractor and Smuggler's Nest's original owner, who sold to a Belgian couple in 1995. It was originally a three-bedroom-with-bathroom affair. Since Johnson's departure, one of the bedrooms has been converted into a study and a TV room.

The dining room is adjacent to a large, well-appointed kitchen and series of open patios.

In the middle of the master bedroom, which has a number of patios, giving a 180-degree view, there is a king-sized, four-poster bed with bamboo poles supporting the canopy. Off the bedroom is a split-level bathroom with a shower, separate "bath for two with a view" and a dressing room. The second bedroom on a lower level has an interior gallery reminiscent of olden days, when minstrels would probably strum their guitars and sing the occupants above to sleep.

Smuggler's Nest's eclectic collection of furnishings include a thick, three-plank rectory-type dining table with a wrought-iron base and an antique Indonesian living set and artefacts, as well as the bamboo-post bed. Each room offers a different experience but privacy is the most precious asset.

Bridget McNamara, who manages the property while the owners are away, has a story to tell about the seclusion of the home. When Johnson had finished building the house, he left the key in the front door. "When he sold the house, ten years later, the key was still there; it had never been out and the house had never been locked."

Right: Smuggler's Nest's open plan takes advantage of the cooling breezes
and views of the ocean and coastline. Designed by Ian Morrison, the house
is built on three levels, with an abundance of patios and lounging areas.

Left: Connecting walkway maintains the outdoor living character of St Lucian hideaway; it's shielded from the elements but never boxed in.

Above: The stark white of the walls contrasts with the dark wood and collectibles. The house is characterised by nooks and alcoves here, there, everywhere.

Below: Indoor-outdoor bathroom area has splendid view from window above sink. Nature's own benevolence is the most important accessory here.

Right: The master bedroom has several patios and a king-size bed with bamboo poles holding up the canopy. The second bedroom is on the lower level.

The dining room is adjacent to the kitchen and a series of open patios, furnished with wooden planter's chairs.

29

Below: This gazebo continues the theme of splendid isolation and overlooks the sea. The other is tucked away in the garden.

Right: The irregularly-shaped pool is ringed by black tiles; the giant trees and surrounding lush greenery complete the illusion that one has stumbled onto a grotto.

THE MAGIC OF
MANDALAY

M U S T I Q U E

An Asian compound in Mustique is as enigmatic as its owner, incorporating glamour,
flair and wit in design, furnishings and gardens

By **Diane Wilson**   Photography by **Mike Toy**

Fear is not an option, this is war! War against the elements, war against the creepy crawlers that would eat an antique table in a day, war against the mundane, the common, the simple, the shoddy. War against the complacency of a house that is "finished". This is war on equanimity and the victor will be unerring excellence.

The giant personality at the centre of this opposition to the ordinary is Felix Dennis. Poet, publisher, host and egoist, the man with the golden touch and a lightning caustic wit, Dennis found Mandalay on the island of Mustique in 1995. It was built in the late Eighties for David Bowie by Arne Hasselqvist, with gardens created by Made Wijaya and interiors conceived by Linda Garland. Together, they created an authentic Asian compound in the Caribbean.

Four-ton stone sculptures mark the entrance to Mandalay, torches spew fire, exotic flowers line pathways and spill from huge vases; nearby, cats lounge on immaculate wooden floors. Infinity pools drain into koi ponds that drain into lotus ponds, giving the illusion that entire rooms are afloat on the water. Every wall and surface is velvety rich wood, yet the house is anything but primitive. High-tech additions are carefully tucked away behind sliding panels and ornate Balinese doors; the kitchen is laden with stainless steel implements and modern weapons of cuisine; the media room is Hollywood-intense with a basket of remote controls that would stump a couch potato technoid and a control panel for the electronic lighting system for the entire property that Bond's Q would covet.

Mandalay has two distinct personas—in daylight, she is a serene sanctuary testament to the Buddhist architecture that inspired her design. It is easy to get away from it all—or your houseguests—at Mandalay. There are countless corners for artistic contemplation, corporate mogul plotting, or naked sun-worshipping. Each bedroom is a cool and comfortable mini suite with private terrace. From the tree house deck, nearby Bequia and St Vincent meet the horizon. In the traditional Balinese gardens, there is seclusion and moments of treasured communes with the gentle nature of the Caribbean.

At night, she is a social watering hole with neon free play Wurlitzer jukeboxes, polished fully-stocked bars, a neon sign announcing the location of the famous Bamboo Lounge, and the ultimate games room. This is a room of toys—a room that brings the 14-year-old boy out in even the most sedate adult. Air hockey, pinball, video games, a computerised dart board, a boxing robot, foosball, play stations, oversized, overstuffed boxing glove lounge chairs and, finally, a glittering show stage equipped with the finest instruments any rock band would long for fill this air-conditioned temple to technology.

Dennis runs his empire from Mandalay for several months each year, and there, he also writes poetry. His most recent book—*Did I Mention the Free Wine*—is into its second printing. He is always accompanied by his longtime companion, Marie-France Demolis. Together, they entertain friends, business associates and family, generously opening Mandalay, a work of excellence in progress, to wide-eyed and happy throngs. This is a house well loved, polished and perfect and never ever complete.

Right: An Indonesian loggia— a bordered, covered colonnade that connects pavilions and rooms lies at the heart of Mandalay. The walls are 19th century carved panels and the columns are oiled teak. It is the preservation of the antique and the love of craftsmanship that elevate Mandalay. The Balinese hand puppets on the end table are over 100 years old.

Left: Ornate drawing room doors were created by a master Balinese craftsman from large and flawless pieces of wood. Beyond the doors is a portion of the loggia, a large continuous deck that rims the koi ponds of the central pavilion.

Right: Call of the wild: from the inverted stallions supporting the glass table to the trompe l'oeil by Mustique resident Jean-Claude Adenin, this drawing room exudes virility.

Tribal visages surprise and intrigue in the Egyptian terrace off the master suite. Each bedroom has a private terrace and access to the pool.

Left: Robinson Crusoe had his tree house and Mandalay has its tree deck. Firmly-cast stilts support this massive conversation pit with a nautilus motif mosaic table.

Above: Mandalay has spectacular gardens. Even the large infinity pool has botanical features central to the design. Mustique's Brittannia Bay is visible below.

GOING UNDERGROUND

G R E N A D A

One man began to build a home on an isolated Grenadian peninsula
but another had to fulfil his mission to bring a fairytale to life

By **Jill Waddell**   Photography by **Alex Smailes**

Mt Hartman Bay Estate is someone's afternoon reverie made a reality. But imagine being able to finish someone else's dream.

Robin Viney, a passionate yachtsman and frequent visitor to the Caribbean, wanted to build a home which met the highest standards of quality and comfort on the island of Grenada. But after his death, it seemed as if his unique architecture designs would be laid to waste.

Viney had started to create something out of a fairytale. The site for the house is on the secluded L'Anse Aux Epines peninsula. Cut into the hillside, the house seems to grow out of the rock. From afar, in the rainy season, Viney's vision seems to retreat into the earth, becoming almost covered in plants and shrubs. This is what 35 to 40 tonnes of steel, chicken wire and a whole lot of concrete molding can produce.

Viney worked on the house for five years but he died in 1998, two years before he could complete it. So who would pick up where the man who dared to dream left off? British businessman Rick Lee felt an instant attraction when he saw the house on the 2.5 acre estate. He said it was architecture that made you smile and he was excited about the shapes and the absence of straight lines. Locally, the house is known as the Underground House or Cave House but it could also be Hobbit House, since it resembles the dwellings of Frodo and friends in Tolkien's *Lord of the Rings*.

The interior surfaces are concave and the ceilings high. While this home has been dug out of the earth, there is still a vastness and openness to the interior. To form the roof, earth was spread back over the concrete structure and a rooftop garden was cultivated. The concrete molding morphed further with its new ownership. A bedroom wing was added, bringing the number of bedrooms to four, and the kitchen moved up a level in the house. The colour of the house also changed; the once earthy tones became a bleached white. Now, the white appears to seep out of the hillside from under the organic rooftop and the entrances look as if they were carved out of white rock formation.

This new white colour contrasts with the deep dark colours of the interior's furnishings. The grand 18-seat dining table is made of interlocking slabs of Brazilian butterfly wing granite, encased by the purpleheart wood. There is a distinct masculinity about the décor with the black settees and wooden furniture. The dark furniture is dramatic against this white canvas and the red Venezuelan tiles.

Surrounding the dug-out of Mt Hartman estate is no beach but a long teak dock with a helipad. Another new addition is the Romeo and Juliet tower. Built alongside the infinity pool, the tower has three levels, with a bedroom crowning the top. The seclusion and the view of the ocean from the tower make it the ultimate destination spot for couples taking in the Grenadian sunrises and sunsets.

Right: British businessman Rick Lee smiled at the challenge of continuing another man's dream, after Robin Viney died before his new home could be completed. One new addition is the Romeo and Juliet tower, built alongside the infinity pool. The tower has three levels, with a bedroom crowning the top.

The 2.5 acre Mt Hartman Bay Estate comprises the main house, which is on three levels, the folly, now a two-bedroom apartment, and a three-bedroom beach house. The upper level includes the main living and entertaining area and kitchen.

Far left: From the outside, the house resembles a fairytale Hobbit house, a ripple of burrows and caves. Inside, it meets the highest standard of modern comfort. The huge 18-seat dining table is made of interlocking slabs of Brazilian granite and purpleheart wood.

Left: This magnificent staircase bordered by an artificial brook blends strong geometry with organic, outdoor elements. The boulders which create a natural, riverine look were hand picked from a variety of sources. The speed of the waterfall is adjustable by the flick of a switch, turning from a fast-flowing river to a meditative stream.

The bathroom is located in the bedroom on the entrance level of the house. There are two showers and a bathub—with the finishings in the warmth of the purpleheart wood. The large oval window gives the bathroom a view of the bay, and with no access to the cliff-side of Mt Hartman the view can be enjoyed with the utmost privacy.

This bedroom is called informally the Blue Room by the owner, but this title is not to describe the bedroom itself but the ultra modern shower that is in the adjacent bathroom. The futuristic capsule-like shower is electric blue. Light streams through the small window into the recently-renovated underground lair.

COLOURS
FOR A
PRIME MINISTER

53

A prime minister's wife honours the past while celebrating her love for colour
at an official government building in St Vincent

Adapted from original article by **Jill Waddell**   Photography by **Alex Smailes**

The biggest challenge for Eloise Gonzalves when re-decorating and renovating Old Montrose was how to control her devotion to colour.

As a historic building, Old Montrose is expected to be perhaps more sedate than her own personality. However, colour is what Caribbean homes are known for and she has not disappointed.

Eloise Harris Gonzalves is the wife of Ralph Gonzalves, prime minister of St Vincent and the Grenadines. The Grenadines comprise 32 small islands, some privately owned, with St Vincent as the largest and most heavily populated. The islands are located just north of Trinidad and Tobago.

While she and her family have made Old Montrose into their private residence since March 2004, it remains an official government building. Gonzalves resolved the colour issue by dividing the house into two areas: private living quarters on the top floor and official entertaining areas below. In the lower entertaining area, Gonzalves used warm, earth tones and for rustic touches, straw baskets and coconut trees stamped on the pillows of the sleek settees. The new wing holds the prime minister's library on the top floor, while on the bottom new addition is the loggia where the prime minister and his wife hold their open-air functions.

In the loggia, Gonzalves will host events of any size, from an intimate sit-down dinner for eight guests to a function for hundreds of dignitaries. But when not concerned with the demands of officialdom, she revels in colour. The top floor's less informal living room has neutral furniture but turquoise pillows, since her aim was to focus on the accents. The most prominent piece of art on display is from Cuba—a painting called "Cane Cutter". Gonzalves points out that her husband's father had gone to cut cane in Cuba decades ago and she felt that the painting was a testament to a Caribbean past. Her daughters' room, which had

once been the official quarters for the previous prime ministers, is now a candy bright room in shades of pink, orange and green.

The floor design accommodates the sunlight and breezes so that they flow from room to room as people might. The master bedroom, despite being situated in the centre of the house, still has access to natural light. The new hallway that now separates the new wing from the master bedroom is cleverly roofed with a skylight. The new wing adds structural and symmetrical balance to the house—and also provides the prime minister with his new library and office quarters.

The library is full of a Prime Minister's treasure: a silver bowl to commemorate the golden jubilee of HM Queen Elizabeth; a replica of Simon Bolivar's sword given to the prime minister by Venezuelan President Hugo Chavez. The bookshelves are overflowing with Caribbean academic literature: the political challenges and histories are logged and stored alphabetically on the dark mahogany shelves. A deep red hue accents the library and helps bring a masculine and formal mood to the large room.

One of the more exciting aspects of the renovation was being able to showcase and rescue pieces of history. The beds in the girls' room are original furniture from when the house was first built. Gonzalves also salvaged a copper, an enormous bowl-like receptacle, once used in sugar production, and turned it into a fountain at the entrance to the house.

More importantly, she discovered the original dining room table was being used as a workman's craft table. Even after seeing its condition and being told that it was of no use, she could not be convinced. The table now sits in the private living quarters of Old Montrose, restored, and no longer hiding under a mass of tools.

This has been the home of Prime Minister Ralph Gonzalves and his family since 2004, when renovations were completed.
It has been divided into two main areas: private living quarters on the top floor and official entertaining areas below.

"Can colour be a mood?" Eloise Gonzalves asks when prompted to describe the mood of her home. In the formal entertaining area downstairs, bursts of turquoise contrast with the softer background palette. Twin recessed nooks hold bouquets, adding more colour and verve to the room.

In the private sitting area upstairs, cool grey is accented by turquoise and lime. The frog on the centre table is a reminder of the Prime Minister's wife's heritage. She is from Dominica, known for its crapaud or "mountain chicken" and amphibian images have a way of winding up in her home. The "Cane Cutter" painting is in the background.

In the Prime Minister's library, overflowing with memorabilia and Caribbean academic literature, poinsettia red accents the neutral tones.

The breakfast gazebo on the top floor is an intimate, sunny nook, where the family can enjoy meals in private. It is separate from the main kitchen and dining areas downstairs.

Below: The master bedroom with its four-poster bed, draped in white, is a study in understated Caribbean elegance. The bedroom is separated from the new wing by a hallway with a skylight.

Right: The Prime Minister's daughter's boudoir is a playland of colour. Candy stripes are repeated in the rug, curtains and pillows.

SOMETHING OLD, SOMETHING NEW

CARRIACOU

A home in the Grenadines, built of wood and stone, is a rich and imaginative blend of traditional and modern

Adapted from original article by **Skye Hernandez**   Photography by **Julie Webster**

Sankofa is an Akan (Ashanti) word meaning, "We should look to the past while moving forward to the future," and is symbolised by a bird in flight with its head turned backwards. It's the name given to a home in Carriacou, owned by African-American businessman Cecil Hollingsworth, and designed by young Grenada architect Bryan Bullen.

Carriacou, just north of Grenada, has just 6,000 inhabitants, a population descended mainly from African slaves and a handful of Scottish sailors. Here, where land and sky meld perfectly with the blue of the Caribbean sea, Sankofa stands as testimony to the richness of the past and hope of the future. It is situated on a gentle slope in the district of Craighton, overlooking the ocean as it stretches northward to Petit Martinque and the other Grenadine islands. From a narrow road, the driveway, bordered by lily ponds, dips down towards the concrete and wood building. Sankofa was built entirely by local artisans and there was generous use of local hardwoods and Carriacou stone.

The building was conceived as a series of pavilions, linked by a continuous wooden balcony. The pavilions house the kitchen, living and sleeping areas and guest room/study.

The owner of the house likens it to an African village—perhaps a collection of small huts whose residents are linked by kinship while the whole compound is enclosed by a wall.

The house itself is approached by a small bridge, connecting the entrance driveway and truss-roofed carport with the veranda.

Bullen had always been fascinated by the Caribbean habit of building homes with verandas (or galleries as they are sometimes called) that face the road, rather than a more private side of the home or a spectacular view. This, he says, is because

of the closeness of Caribbean community life; people call out as they pass by, sometimes dropping in for a while or to share a meal.

The veranda at Sankofa has a public side but wraps around the house to afford privacy on the sea side. From the street, the house seems fairly enclosed but the opposite side opens wide through louvred wooden doors to take in the expanse of sea and sky. The cantilevered balconies create the effect of a house built right over the water and just under the sky.

Bullen sees the design of Sankofa as bringing together the traditional Caribbean great house and chattel house. There are no grand rooms in Sankofa but instead a series of intimate living spaces—several chattel houses, if you will, made into one plantation house.

Pigmented concrete is used over much of the building, giving it a rich, ochre colour. Wood rafters, louvres, doors and walls complement the earthy tones. Translucent white awnings shade the balconies and offer a gentle glow in the afternoon sun.

The kitchen is a stunning example of the manipulation of colour and light. Lemon-green walls contrast with the dark wood of the heavy carved door from India and its translucent corrugated roof brings the blue sky down into the heart of the building. Bullen relied on indigenous materials because he wanted the house to appear to emerge from its site rather than sit on top of it.

The home is furnished with African and Indian furniture, art objects and fabrics, as well as some quirky antique pieces of sentimental value. There are many personal touches: shells collected from the beach; a playful mural; and even a piece of brick from Mrs Hollingsworth's late grandmother's house embedded in the wall at the entrance.

Sankofa is designed as a series of pavilions joined by walkways. The house is approached by a small bridge connecting the entrance driveway and truss-roofed carport with the veranda.

Below: A translucent corrugated roof in the kitchen lets the sunshine in but it has a strong UV coating. Like all other rooms, the kitchen looks out to the sea side of the house. The carved door is from India, a tribute to the ancestry of the owner's Grenada-born wife.

Right: The lemon and lime of the kitchen sing against the cobalt blue of the adjoining living space and warmth of the wooden African furniture. There are no grand rooms at Sankofa but a series of intimate living spaces, like several chattel houses made into one plantation.

Right: Sunlight streams into the bathroom and the window gives the illusion of an open-air outdoor bathing nook.

Far right: The entrance to Sankofa, looking through the driveway. From the street, the building seems enclosed but on the opposite side, its wooden louvred doors are flung open to embrace the expanse of sea and sky.

HOUSE OF BRICK AND STONE

ST LUCIA

A retired executive builds retreat from volcanic rock and celebrates space,
light and air amidst the fabled Twin Pitons of St Lucia

Adapted from original article by **Garry Steckles**   Photography by **Julie Webster**

When Norman Brick awakens at Tamarind House and the twin Pitons are swathed in sunlight, with the Caribbean Sea to his right and the island's lush green hills to the left, he considers himself a very fortunate man.

Brick, who was born in England, built his home amidst two towering green pyramids in St Lucia, the fabled Twin Pitons. While the design and style are anything but traditional West Indian, Tamarind House embraces the priorities that were in place when craftsmen of a bygone age were defining what is now known as Caribbean style. Space, light and air were the most important considerations in the creation of the 14,000-square-foot home.

Brick, former vice president in the United States for what became Eastman Kodak, undertook the construction of Tamarind House from 1978 to 1980. When he retired in 1980, he spent another 10 years as a consultant in Hungary, Brazil and Czechoslovakia, before devoting most of his time to soaking up the view from Tamarind House.

The walls of his home were constructed from local Belfond stone and Wayne Brown, a Canadian who came to St Lucia in the Sixties and who specialises in building one-of-a-kind properties, recalls how the local masons would sit under the tamarind tree on the property, chipping away at the pink, grey and fawn volcanic rocks. The ceiling was crafted from Guyanese greenheart wood, the doors from red cedar in Brown's carpentry shop in Soufriere, and the floors were made from terra cotta tiles from Barbados. Large wallaba poles, which were also used as beams across the rooms, supported the roof rafters.

The design centrepiece of the house is the living room and terrace, covering about 2,500 square feet. The living room is sparingly but exquisitely furnished with Caribbean and French period pieces. The uncluttered terrace is shaded by trees and there is but a scattering of tables and chairs.

An arched doorway leads directly to the living room with its vast ceiling. The arches in the living room were re-done three times before Brick and Brown were satisfied with their curves and height. A flight of stone stairs descends to an open courtyard with banana trees and a large, spreading tamarind. A spacious kitchen and three bedrooms adjoin the living room. The two main bedrooms, each with private verandas, face south and consist of only three walls with doors. Nothing is allowed to obstruct the view of the Pitons.

Perhaps nothing reflects Brick's determination to make the most of his home with a view than his bathroom. It's modest in size but the doors open to reveal, once again, the mighty Pitons.

A short stroll from the main building is the cottage and lodge, each self-contained and spacious. They are used to accommodate visiting friends and relatives. A BioFlex-surfaced tennis court, which Brick laughingly describes as an expensive mistake, and a rectangular swimming pool, each on a different level, complete what must be one of the most unusual homes in the region.

Much of the furniture at Tamarind House are antiques, such as the tables, armoires and chaises longues, which were bought in Soufriere and reflect the period when St Lucia was under French control. Several pieces came from the Golden Lemon in St Kitts and a large armoire in the living room was imported from France. The living room sofas and the large trestle dining table were made out of wild breadfruit wood in Brown's carpentry shop, while other unique pieces were made by St Lucian craftsmen, most notably master carpenter Harris Lionel.

Previous page: Original art adorns nearly every wall of the St Lucian home of English-born Norman Brick, where furnishings are spare but comfortable. His artistic nature is not surprising, considering he spent much of his life as a Kodak executive.

Left: Antique furniture, cool red tiles and white bedding create an airy, understated elegance, which is evident throughout Tamarind House. The home has three bedrooms adjoining the main living area. The two main bedrooms consist of only three walls; nothing is allowed to block the view of the Pitons.

Left and below: An arched doorway leads to the living room, which is so open to the terrace, they seem like a single unit. The living room and the uncluttered terrace are the design centrepiece of the house. The living room furniture and the large trestle dining table were made out of wild breadfruit wood, while the period pieces were made by St Lucian craftsmen.

Above: A tamarind tree provides shade in the large, open circular courtyard. While the design and style of the 14,000-square foot property is anything but traditional West Indian, the philosophy behind Tamarind House embraces the priorities that were in place in a bygone era. Space, light and air are the main assets.

Right: From the veranda, Norman Brick has a priceless view of the mighty Pitons. They rise majestically from the ocean and seem to pierce the sky. In the morning, this mountainside home and the Pitons are bathed in sunlight, with the Caribbean Sea to the right and the lush green hills to the left.

JUST SAY
AAAAH!

MUSTIQUE

From the gold leaf bed fit for a sultan's palace to the infinity pool to the magnificent Mirador,
Toucan Hill is an ode to living life to the fullest

By **Diane Wilson**   Photography by **Mike Toy**

On the very crest of the highest hill on the southwestern shore of the Grenadine island of Mustique is a Moorish house that makes you say ahhhhh. Toucan Hill is fantasy in construct, built and designed by Tatiana Copeland for herself and for her husband Gerret. For many years, the Copelands holidayed on Mustique and came to know each of the 75 architectural confections on the island. They decided what they liked, what worked, and eventually knew what they had to have in their own Mustique island home.

The style of this Moorish castle is much a matter of function as one of taste. The Copelands wanted a fantasy, but one that would stand up to hundreds of hot, sunny, breezy days, the occasional hurricane and tropical humidity. For nearly ten years, craftsmen sculpted concrete, laid flourishes of exotic Turkish tiles, and cultivated acres of garden.

The result: Ali Baba's Arabian Nights on a tropical island.

The owners' private wing is the suite of a king and queen: a cool blue infinity pool extends beyond the private terrace. Inside, a glittering gold leaf king-size custom bed and matching bedside tables dominate. The dressing room-bath is also swabbed in gold that sparkles against thousands of tiny, highly-polished onyx tiles.

One of the most striking features of Toucan Hill is its Mirador. From there, in moments of peaceful repose, guests glimpse fragments of distant sails glinting across the sea, or let their gaze fall into a brilliant fiery Caribbean sunset, or curl up under the brilliance of the Milky Way on star gazing mats. Outdoor lighting is subtle: hundreds of candles, votives and tiki torches are lit at twilight, marking paths and pools throughout the property.

Dinner in the spectacular dining pavilion offers sparkling views of the sea and the infinity pool. As ingenious as the mirror room of Jaipur's Amber Palace, this round gazebo was skillfully finished to match the surrounding seas and sky. Custom paint, flecked with silver, reflects light and makes the delicate blue walls and sky-painted ceiling disappear. The floor is a sea blue marble mosaic tile and the table, a delicate Indian mother of pearl inlay.

Courtyard gardens, complete with mature palm trees and walls of blooming bougainvillea, punctuate the property. Feather grass, jasmine, alamanda, lady of the night, firecracker and portulaca are just a few of the flowers and ornamental plants in abundance at Toucan Hill. The Cloister room and indoor gardens are decidedly Moroccan—complete with columns, mosaics and two fountains. This is an outdoor room in harmony with the garden and the skies. As in Morocco, rainwater from adjacent rooftops is channelled there, creating a crystalline waterfall of rain.

The Great Room plays to the senses with texture, colour and scent. Tables from Agra, chandeliers, fabrics and ceramics collected in Turkey, Morocco, India and Bali create the illusion of a sultan's palace.

Four spacious and luxurious guest suites are tucked away in discrete and quiet corners. Each has a different theme, each its own personality, and all have double terraces, command delicious views and have large living spaces. Tuareg blue on accents on white, golden walls the shade of Sahara sand, muted tones of sunset and water are used extensively in four fabulous suites.

This exuberant ode to friends, luxury, fantasy and romance, Toucan Hill is a celebration of life well lived.

Right: The private terrace off the master suite offers a solitary southern view of the jewel hues of the Caribbean Sea.

Left: The dining gazebo is furnished to match the surrounding seas and sky. The walls are flecked with silver to reflect light. The floor is sea-blue marble mosaic tile and the table, Indian mother of pearl inlay.

Right: Each of the four guest suites is spacious, luxurious and serene. Each has a different theme and each has a terrace and commanding view of earth and sky.

Left: The Great Room is a gateway to a magical land. Tables from Agra, fabrics and ceramics from Turkey, Morocco, India and Bali contribute to the illusion of a sultan's palace. The silver coffee table was once an Indian gate.

Below: The Sultan Suite, in deep russet and rust, is the grandest of the four guest suites. Inlaid mirrors, ornate cushions and brass lanterns are of Indian origin.

Left: An opulent king-size gold leaf bed dominates the owners' suite. A cool blue infinity pool extends beyond the private terrace. The Copelands wanted fantasy when they created their Moorish castle and this room meets the standard:Arabian Nights on a tropical island.

Below: The master bathroom is swabbed in gold that sparkles against thousands of tiny, highly-polished onyx tiles.

Left: Wicker furniture is placed for conversation. The views are not limited to the sea or extensive gardens, as an antique Turkish tile mosaic graces an otherwise stark white wall.
Below: This fountain is in a magnificent tiled courtyard, leading to the lush gardens of Toucan Hill.

TEAK FOR TWO

SAINT BARTHELEMY

An architect's dream house in Saint Barthelemy is crafted in Javanese teak and other exotic woods

Adapted from original article by **Ellen Lampert Greaux**   Photography by **Julie Webster and Fred Burnier**

Architect Philippe Stouvenot and his wife Ghislaine Rey had been living on Saint Barthelemy for just five years when they decided it was time to put down roots in the rocky soil of the French Caribbean island.

About four years ago, they completed the building of Villa Safari, made primarily of benkirai teak imported from Java, and strategically placed to capture incredible sweeping views, and the light breezes that waft across their hillside.

"There are fantastic views everywhere," says Stouvenot, looking out at the commanding 180-degree views of the Atlantic Ocean and the hills and valleys of the island. "The more open a house is, the more you can enjoy the views." Villa Safari, an open, inviting two-bedroom, two-bathroom house, has a large salon that is more like a covered terrace than an enclosed room. A small pool, tiled in deep blue, sits at the edge of the salon, and is flanked by a covered dining area on one side and a bedroom on the other, with a lacy white hammock suspended right next to the pool.

The house remains cool in the afternoon because of the wood. A few concrete walls peek out from the wood in the kitchen and the bathrooms, which are used to anchor the house to the hillside. "We also like the contemporary look of the concrete painted white," Rey says. "It softens things up." The wood on the inside of the house has been treated with teak oil. In contrast, the wood on the exterior, including such exotic woods as merbau and ipe, has been left to age and is turning to a soft shade of silvery grey.

The wooden house is like a large puzzle. Originally built in Bali, it was taken apart, the pieces numbered, put into containers and shipped to St Barth, where local carpenters put the house back together. The cool grey tones of the stone walls blend smoothly with the warm tones of the wood, and contrast with the bright red bougainvillea that tumbles over the walls.

Windows in the bedroom on the main living level have wooden shutters that let the air flow freely while also filtering the sun. "They can be closed completely to block out the light completely," Rey adds. "This is great for an afternoon nap and you can wake up as twilight arrives and lights start to twinkle across the island."

The furniture is an eclectic mix of modern and antique. A large Balinese day bed, made of teak, serves as a sofa and occupying the central area of the living room. It is upholstered in off-white with a multitude of brightly-striped pillows in yellow, pink, orange, red and white adding a burst of colour to the room. A traditional planter's chair contrasts with a pair of contemporary wooden chairs with a humorous trompe l'œil design.

Contemporary tables of wood and stainless steel by French architect Jean Nouvel stand not too far from a bookcase from India made of heavily carved wood. A four-poster bed, made in Bali, is draped with mosquito netting. In the kitchen, two islands are topped with blue granite from Brazil; the granite is also used for a large square dining table, surrounded by stainless steel mesh chairs.

"Safari means voyages in the Swahili language," says Rey. "We are people who love to travel." This wanderlust is reflected throughout the house, where large sculptures in wood and stone and African masks represent voyages to the far corners of the world. Paintings and photographs by contemporary artists complete the collection.

Patios, paved with smooth river stones from Bali, surround the house, and include a barbecue area off the kitchen. And outdoors, just off the bathroom, there is one last surprise—an outdoor shower, where when stripped down, one can truly feel close to Nature.

Previous pages: A lacy, white hammock is suspended next to the pool, an ideal place to relax and take advantage of the cool breezes. The house has a contemporary look which blends well with the Bali theme. Stainless steel mesh chairs surround granite dining table on the terrace.

Above: A large square dining table, made of blue granite from Brazil, is surrounded by stainless steel mesh chairs. The granite is also used for two islands in the open, airy kitchen.

Right: Much of the furniture in the house was custom-made in Bali. A large, Balinese day bed, made of teak, serves as a sofa in the living room. The white seats provide neutral background for lots of brightly-striped pillows, adding punches of colour to the room.

Far left: Bright red bougainvillea blooms contrast with the warm Javanese teak of Villa Safari, strategically placed on a hillside to capture the soothing breezes and views of ocean, hills and valleys.

Center: The second bedroom on the lower level doubles as an office and has sliding glass doors, so the homeowners can work in air-conditioned comfort while soaking up the splendid views.

Left: The entrance to Villa Safari, leading to the open living area. The cool grey of the local stone blends with the warm tones of the Javanese wood.

99

Above: The bathroom leads to an outdoor shower. Inside, double face basins mimic large bowls and baskets provide under-counter storage. Indoors and out, the house is designed to fit the environment. The architect describes himself as an architectural chameleon.

Right: The outdoor shower is a delightful surprise off the bathroom. But it is in keeping with the tropical, close-to-Nature mood of the entire house, which is surrounded by patios paved with smooth river stones from Bali.

THIS GREAT
OLD HOUSE

JAMAICA

An ancient Jamaican home is restored to glory, down to the wooden tub and antique staircase

Adapted from original article by **Mirah Lim**   Photography by **Cookie Kinkead**

Set in the hills of Trelawny overlooking the north coast of Jamaica, Arcadia is the weekend home of Heinz and Elisabeth Simonitsch. The Austrian couple, famed for their involvement with Montego Bay's prestigious Half Moon Resort, has carefully restored this old great house, which was built in 1832. "We have a love affair with this house. It's been a lot of hard work, but it's finally got to the stage where we really enjoy it," says Elisabeth.

Built from local limestone quarried nearby the property, the initial house was a one-storey Georgian bungalow with two wings to the east and west of the main building. Twenty years after it was constructed, a prosperous plantation owner named William Sewell bought Arcadia. Over the following 100 years the house remained in the Sewell family, passing from generation to generation. Each new owner made additions and renovations to the original structure, and in time, the house grew to a two-storey building with a wraparound veranda. The veranda was decorated with intricate cast iron fretwork, specially shipped as ballast from Glasgow, Scotland. A terrace and exterior bathroom were also added to the house in the late 19th century. In the 1940s, an upper floor with three bedrooms was also constructed onto the west wing.

In 1973, William Sewell's great-grandson sold Arcadia to Heinz Simonitsch, the then Managing Director of Half Moon Golf, Tennis and Beach Club. When Heinz bought Arcadia, the ravages of time's passing marked the house. But the Simonitschs have gone through, room by room, clearing out, stripping down, repairing, repainting and refurbishing. "I don't like to throw away anything. I have kept most of what we've found at the house, even some things that others would say is junk," says Elisabeth. "Eighty per cent of the furniture belonged to the Sewells and the rest are Jamaican antiques that we have bought"

Made mostly from cut limestone and wood, the house has a high, shingled roof and mahogany, tile or stone floors. In addition to the three bedrooms on the main house's second floor, there is also a private study and formal living room. The wraparound upper veranda features spectacular views of the Jamaican coastline and the distant cockpit mountains, framed by the elaborate iron fretwork. The first and second floors are connected by a regal wooden staircase, held together in the old-fashioned way with wooden bolts instead of nails. "This staircase may be the only one like it left in Jamaica," says Elisabeth, as she descends from the second storey into the central hallway on the lower level. The hallway runs from the porte-cochere to the back garden and pool terrace. To the east of the hallway rests the grand dining room, while the downstairs living room and study lie on the west.

Facing the mountains, the back of house has a terrace that opens onto a swimming pool and jacuzzi. Arcadia's first bathroom sits just off the terrace, and still holds the original wooden tub, now equipped with a modern shower head. Nearby, in another room, is the old three-seater wooden toilet. Together, these rooms made up Arcadia's bathroom facilities in the late 19th century. "Everything still works," remarks Elisabeth as she passes the old bathrooms, "although I am not sure why you'd want to try it."

But, by far, the most unusual room in the house is the old cellar, lying beneath the west wing. The Simonitschs have transformed the cellar into an in-house pub with its own bar and lounge, and antique organ. The room's low ceiling is lined with hand-hewn wooden beams while the floor is covered in red bricks. Elisabeth also has on display some of the old bottles, planks of wood and other items she found buried at the house. Yet, the most haunting reminder of Arcadia's history is the gun hole, a small slit in one of the cellar's walls, once used as a form of defence in times of rebellion.

Previous page: Cane rockers and lounge chairs line the veranda, like sentinels to history.

Left: From the upper storey, one can view the Jamaican coastline and the distant cockpit mountains, framed by the elaborate ironwork.

Right: At the side of the house, garden benches, wooden louvres and a painting add unexpected detail.

Far left: The intricate cast iron fretwork of the veranda was specially shipped from Glasgow, Scotland in Henry Sewell's 300-ton barque. The house was first a one-storey Georgian bungalow with two wings to the east and west of the main building. Twenty years after it was constructed, plantation owner William Sewell bought Arcadia. Over the following 100 years, the house remained in the Sewell family but each new owner made renovations to the original structure, and in time the house grew to a two-storey building with the wraparound veranda.

Left: Like lace on the hem of a lady's gown, the ironwork at the top of the posts adds an elegant detail to the ancient Jamaican great house.

Left: The former kitchen, with its old brick oven, fireplace and brick walls, has been converted into a cosy and casual dining room. The owners stripped away all the plaster and found the brick walls underneath. Above the dining table, a skylight helps to keep the room bright and airy.

Below: The most intriguing room in the house is probably the cellar, which has been transformed into a pub with its own bar and lounge. The low ceiling is lined with hand-hewn planks of wood and the floor is ancient, uneven red brick. It's like being in the womb of history.

Right: Arcadia's bathroom facilities in the 19th century consisted of a small building behind the house, containing an enormous cedar tub. Rainwater was collected and poured into the tub. There was also a wooden three-seater toilette. It's all been preserved and everything still works, although the rest of the house is equipped with modern plumbing.

Far right: Four-poster bed brings grandeur to the room and the warmth of the wooden floors provides a cosiness. Remaining faithful to the history of Arcadia, the owners filled Arcadia with Jamaican antiques and kept much of the interior furnishings inherited from the generations of Sewells who lived in Arcadia for about a century.

Right: The first and second floors are connected by a swirling wooden staircase, held together in the old-fashioned way with wooden bolts instead of nails. It may well be the only one of its kind left in Jamaica.

Far right: Facing the mountains, the back of house has a terrace that opens onto a swimming pool and jacuzzi. Arcadia's first bathroom, added in the late 19th century, sits just off the terrace.

Arcadia, made mostly from limestone quarried on the common near the house, replaced an older building, which stood at the peak of the ridge, overlooking the sea and was probably destroyed by fire or storm. Emma and Horace Sewell undertook the renovations of the 1940s. They lie buried near the site of the original house. In 1973, Horace's sole surviving son, Geoffrey, sold Arcadia to Heinz Simonitsch.

Royal palms line the driveway to Arcadia, which has survived hurricanes and the ravages of time.

PIETERMAAI 154

C U R A Ç A O

A couple puts faith in the development of a historic district in Curacao
and finds a jewel of Dutch colonial architecture

Adapted from original article by **Skye Hernandez**   Photography by **Sean Drakes**

From the street, the house at Pietermaai 154 seems like a charming bungalow, albeit with a wide swath of staircase leading to the front door. Walk up those stairs and one begins to understand a whole different scale, one that's much grander than the first impression, though no less appealing.

The heavy wooden doors lead to a generous living room, as cool and dark as the corridor beyond it—open to the sky—is light and sunny. Exploring the home with owners Willem Van Bokhost and his wife, Barbara, reveals a jewel of 19th century Dutch colonial architecture, updated to accommodate the modern lifestyle of a couple that has exquisite, yet simple, taste, and many friends to entertain. What first seemed like a relatively small bungalow set far back from the street is actually built on three levels, with living areas that stretch all the way to the sea at the back. A house, it seems, with a place for every mood.

The Pietermaai district where Willem and Barbara live is part of Curaçao's historic capital, Willemstad, listed by Unesco as a World Hertiage Site, for its cultural importance to all the world's peoples. Pietermaai runs eastwards from the downtown core of Punda along the border of the Caribbean Sea. It was the first area that Portuguese-Jewish merchants moved to when they began to outgrow Punda. Until a few years ago, the district could be considered "depressed". In fact, when Willem bought the house in 1990, he says he was considered the first "fool" to take such a risk.

"It made sense to me because it was near downtown but built in an area that was expansive and picturesque. I thought all I had to do was wait a few years and it would become a good area for business and for living-and so it has turned out to be."

The full restoration began in 1993. "The house was originally one storey plus an attic," says Willem. "After we bought it, we decided to excavate the crawling spaces under the house and make a storage room and bar there, and the apartment." The front part of the house, the entrance and living room areas, remained mostly unchanged.

With the help of Dutch architect Anko van der Woude, the seaward-facing side of the house was changed significantly to create what is now a luxurious swimming pool and deck area. "We moved the old maid's quarters at the back of the house, and threw out endless junk from the back," explains Willem. The garage at the side of the building was also demolished. The roof of the building was raised to create two bedrooms and a modern bathroom upstairs, where before there was only the attic. Two guest rooms, a sewing room and bathroom flank the tiled corridor, as do a neat kitchen and dining room.

The house at Pietermaai 154 is believed to have been built by Benjamin Suares between 1858 and 1873. Willem says that according to the register of mortgages in 1873, there was a residence, two small dwellings and some other buildings on the property. Two wings at the back of the house were added later. In 1906, Eduard Salomon Lansberg acquired the house and lived there with his two daughters. Daughter Editha Lansberg died in 1989, having willed the property to the United Dutch-Portuguese Israel Community, the "Mikvé Israel-Emanuel". Willem was able to buy the house because of ancestral links to the Jewish community.

Willem says that if he were renovating the house at Pietermaai 154 now—with new, stricter regulations—he would not be able to make some of the changes he did, but he's justifiably pleased with the way the home has been preserved with historical integrity, while complementing a modern lifestyle.

The grand entrance to the house owned by Willem Van Bokhost and his wife, Barbara. While excavating the area below the house, workers discovered a box with some tiles, with an address that helped them trace the original manufacturer to Belgium. They were then able to replace all the damaged tiles on this staircase and inside the house with used tiles from old buildings in Belgium. The home, painted green with yellow highlights, is set a fair distance from the road, giving it the feel of a large bungalow, rather than a three-storey house.

Left: *The formal living room is part of the original house built in the late 19th-century; this is a reading nook in the minimally furnished room. Dark wood and deep red are offset by cream-coloured Indian silk curtains made by Barbara herself. The antique furniture in the living room is of Curaçao wood, made by local woodworkers.*

Above: *Apple figurines add colourful, quirky detail in living room. All furnishings were carefully selected to complement the ancient character of the house.*

123

124

Left: The white guest room opens out with shuttered windows on to the sunny corridor. Crisp linen, gossamer curtains and whimsical craft create a playful, relaxed ambience.

Right: The tiled corridor is opened to the sky and the elements (it doesn't rain much in Curaçao). This view is from outside the kitchen looking towards the living room to the street-side of the property. The two bedrooms and a bath that were created when the roof was raised are upstairs.

Left: The compact kitchen is adjacent to the formal dining room, in the background. There is also a casual entertaining area, furnished with wood and wicker pieces, that looks out to the deck and ocean; this room is at the seaside end of the corridor, next to the dining room.

Right: While excavating the area below the house, workers discovered a box with some tiles, with an address that helped them trace the original manufacturer to Belgium. The owners bought the house in 1990 and the full restoration began in 1993.

Left: The basement bar, complete with pool table and atmospheric lighting, is in a cave-like area that's a world of its own. Air-conditioned and cosy now, this was one of the areas that Willem Van Bokhost discovered when he bought the house. It was full of rubble and had to be excavated–this bar, a storeroom and a separate apartment were created out of the rubble.

Above: At the end of this tiled corridor lies an informal entertaining area, then a few stairs leading to the outdoors and the pool area. On one side of the corridor lie the kitchen, white guest bedroom and formal dining room and on the other, a bathroom and sewing room.

PARADISE REGAINED

B A R B A D O S

German travellers find a new paradise in Barbados and turn it into a collector's dream and a retreat for friends and family

Adapted from original article by **Neysha Soodeen**   Photography by **Bob kiss**

After two and a half years of searching for a new home, Rene Margies and Matthias Servais found two acres of land on the West Coast of Barbados which fulfilled all five of their requirements: it was on a ridge overlooking the ocean; there were old trees; the terrain was undulating; it was private; and it was close to the beach.

Margies and Servais have settled into their haven for more than a decade, after fleeing their beloved 25-acre coconut estate plantation in Sri Lanka because of political unrest. They called their new home Cane Heaven.

Servais, an interior designer, wanted to recreate the plantation style architecture with high ceilings and maximum ventilation. The entire front of the house at Cane Heaven is open to a never-ending view of the pool, cane fields and the blue of the Caribbean sky. Servais kept the east and west sides of the house open, added louvre windows to all the other walls, allowing virtually no direct sunlight to enter the house. He also designed the house to accommodate the larger pieces of furniture which he and Margies had brought from Sri Lanka and Switzerland. The friends had travelled extensively while operating their own import-export company.

The expansive living room contains a wonderful mix of West Indian, Asian and European furniture. The wicker living room set, designed by Servais himself, was made in China. Behind the seating, two cabinets stand guard over the living area. The Almeira cabinet with jackwood and ebony wood carvings is a Sri Lankan masterpiece from the Dutch period. The other cabinet was bought in Europe and houses Servais's collection of Buddhas. On either side of the seating area are two Balinese umbrellas, held by two Nubian Boys, which Margies says "serve absolutely no purpose but liven up the huge space".

Cane Heaven's veranda spans the entire width of the house and has two seating areas, with outdoor living and dining rooms just beyond their formal counterparts. The wicker furniture on the veranda was also designed by Servais. "I specially designed these seats to that our cats can sit on the arms of the chairs and curl up while we are sitting down," he says. In the outdoor dining area, an Almeira chest is flanked by two antique Baroque angels acquired in Portugal. The chandelier hanging from the veranda ceiling is one of a set of four from Bellerive, the Barbados home of the late Hollywood star Claudette Colbert.

Perhaps the most intriguing feature indoors is the staircase, designed to curve around a statue they bought in Paris, which is called The Negro Man. Opposite the sculpture is a seating area with an ebony couch and table. On the right are elaborate Phillipine gravestones.

The first floor has two rooms, the master bedroom and a guest bedroom, called the Mola Room, dedicated to their collection of molas from Panama. Molas are the blouses worn by the Cuna Indian women and are decorated with a reversal appliqué of up to seven or eight layers of fabric carefully sewn together. The layers are cut and tucked under to reveal the colours beneath.

Servais and Margies began collecting molas from the San Blas islands and also from collectors in Sweden, Germany and the United States. Across the hall from the Mola Room is the master bedroom, with an amazing collection of 16th and 18th century santos (saint figurines) from the Phillipines and a 1723 painting of Johan Sebastian Bach.

Across the hall from the Mola Room is the master bedroom which has one intriguing feature—it doubles as a living room. The area was designed with a huge lounge area to the front, which takes advantage of the ocean view.

Servais's rationale is this: "A bedroom costs the same amount to build and decorate as any other part of the house, so why not make more use out of it. When we have guests over, they invariably climb to this floor to experience the spectacular view."

133

Previous page: The staircase was designed to accommodate "The Negro Man," which Matthais Servais bought in Paris. Opposite is a seating area with an ebony and cane couch and side table. Up the stairs, the walls are covered with Haitian and Barbadian art, the one exception being a painting by Servais himself.

Left: The master bedroom is huge, incorporating a lounge area with an ocean view. "A bedroom costs the same amount to build and decorate as any other part of the house, so why not make more use out of it?" says Servais.

Above: Formal dining room has a touch of wild-animal-patterned seats. The chandelier is one of a set of four from Bellerive, the Barbados home of the late Hollywood star, Claudette Colbert. The contents of the house could not be sold separately at the estate auction, but knowing that Servais and Margies loved the chandeliers, the people who bought Bellerive gave them the set, on the condition that they never sell them and they always remain at Cane Heaven.

The master bedroom doubles as a lounge and one might even call it an art gallery. Above the bed is a collection of 16th and 18th century saint figurines from the Phillipines and a 1723 painting of Bach.

The Mola Room is dedicated to a collection of molas, blouses worn by the Cuna Indian women of Panama. The pale walls and the white beds and curtains provide a stark backdrop for the colourful molas. The owners had their first of four exhibitions of mola art in Switzerland in 1978.

Below: Cane Heaven's veranda spans the entire width of the house with outdoor living and dining rooms located just outside their formal interior counterparts. The wicker furniture was designed by Servais with a special purpose, "so that our cats can sit on the arms of the chairs and curl up while we are sitting down."

Right: The gazebo on the edge of the property is decorated with wicker furniture and an antique English brass bed, overflowing with bright pillows and draped in Indian fabric. The lantern is from Claudette Colbert's Chinese gazebo and was given to her by Ronald Tree, the original owner of Sandy Lane estate. Beyond the gazebo lie the lush gardens and views of the cane fields and ocean.

Left: The greenhouse is twice the size of the one Rene Margies had in Sri Lanka. Here, he grows orchids, lilies, alocasias, begonias and ferns. There are also two ponds, one containing arium water plants from the Amazon River and the other a waterfall, with giant clams from Cebu Island as part of the design.

Above: Cane Heaven on the west coast of Barbados sits on a ridge overlooking the ocean. The owners have poured a lifetime of experience, travel and style into their two-acre paradise.

COLLECTOR'S CASTLE

T R I N I D A D

Every woman's home is her castle and this style queen reigns from an unusual two-storey kingdom,
which hearkens to olden days but is brimming with new and exciting ideas

Adapted from original articles by **Sharon Millar** and **Neysha Soodeen**   Photography by **Alex Smailes**

Kathryn Stollmeyer Wight is the sort of woman who would take something new and make it look 100 years old. She would rather spend money on a rock than a pair of new shoes. And her plates on the dinner table never match.

Her home, in a breezy valley in western Trinidad, looks like a fairytale cottage, with its gingerbread details, demerara windows and vibrant colours. And it is always changing. "Your taste changes so much as time goes by and the things you collect throughout the years add to your home," Wight explains.

She has tried mirrors at the bottom of a pond to reflect light and on one occasion, she planted among the heliconias, a wooden garden figure, named Sugars, who was all bewigged and bespectacled. His costumes were changed frequently, depending on the mood of the house.

The house was designed by her architect brother, Allan Stollmeyer, and Wight told him she wanted it to look and feel as if it had been around for a century. She also wanted to conjure up memories of her idyllic childhood in the Santa Cruz valley, where she bathed in a river and enjoyed the sound of rain on a corrugated tin roof. The poolside garden, in particular, reminds her of country living. It is always a work in progress and becomes more and more charismatic over the years. The crowning piece is a gazebo, built of greenheart and teak and designed for entertaining with its rooftop terrace.

The built-in barbeque and bar area are unobtrusive and the space keeps its charm with brightly-painted demerara windows and a whimsical stencil that softens the large wooden beams. In the ceiling, tin sheeting has been laid between the rafters. Hanging stainless steel lights run in two parallel lines down the centre of the ceiling, with each emitting a pinpoint of light, like fireflies. A climb up the stairs to the rooftop takes one into the canopy of the overhanging samaan tree. There, among the wild bromeliads, is where Kathi and husband Gregory often have dinner, overlooking the pool. Large samaans, black olives and cassias surround

the poolside area below. The garden looks as if it evolved effortlessly but considerable detail went into its development. The artfully-placed river boulders that peep from behind large elephant ear shrubs have had their velvety mossy surfaces assisted along by the daily application of yoghurt.

This attention to detail and Wight's creativity are evident throughout the home. Her daughter Ada Kate jokingly calls it an imitation house, since "everything is made to look like something else". The floors are concrete made to look like tile; the coral stone is not real; and the "wooden" panels outside the house are also made of concrete. Wight chose concrete because she wanted the floors to be cool and steel poles were used to indent the concrete to create the tiled effect.

A unifying feature is the uninhibited use of colour. The breakfast room, a cheerful alcove that adjoins the main kitchen area, has stable doors leading to the outdoor veranda and a large porch area. The doors, lime green bordered in prussian blue, frame the natural outdoor display of trees and flowers. The vermilion powder room on the ground floor is legendary.

Her daughters' rooms follow an Indian theme, with a dramatic pairing of brass and silk, dark woods and bright colours. The saffron walls in Ada Kate's room and hot fuschia in Sophie's present the perfect backdrop for the ornate wooden furniture and brass accessories. Sophie's bedroom has the added details of a vaulted, royal purple ceiling and a heavily-worked, brass-framed mirror. Also, a richly-textured silk sari has been cleverly used as an elaborate window treatment.

Wight is a collector and her home is full of family photographs, art work and memorabilia, including her report card from when she was nine. About 80 black and white family photographs fill the walls at the top of the stairs.

A perfect example of what Wight considers important in turning a house into a home is a framed sheet of paper, displayed in the kitchen. It reads, "Gone to have a baby, be back on Monday," written from Wight to her housekeeper.

Previous page: Designed by architect Allan Stollmeyer for his sister Kathi Stollmeyer Wight and her husband Gregory Wight, this gingerbread house in western Trinidad looks like a fairytale cottage. Kathi wanted it to look as if it were 100 years old and she also wanted to conjure up memories of her childhood in the scenic Santa Cruz valley.

Far left: Above the staircase is a gallery of memories. Black and white family photographs line the red walls, including some of Kathi's late parents, Jeffrey, a West Indies cricketer, and his wife, Sarah. Kathi's favourite photograph is of Gregory's great-grandfather smiling at Gregory's grandfather embracing Gregory's father.

Left: The legendary vermilion powder room, where artwork and family memorabilia cover the walls, including the moving announcement celebrating the Wights' arrival in their new home and a 1961 letter to the Trinidad Guardian. "I collect everything and throw away nothing," Kathi says. "I have my report card from when I was nine and all of the children's teeth."

147

Left: Every month or so, the homeowner buys a single plate to add to her collection. None of the plates on her dinner table match and a the table setting might include calabash gourds as soup bowls and a leaf as a butter dish.

Right: Her daughter's room follows an Indian theme, with purple and fuchsia walls, brass and silk accessories and elephant details everywhere. Mirrored decals make up an eye-catching border. Colour, the uninhibited, passionate use of colour, is the home's unifying feature.

Left: The outdoor dining area has brightly-painted Demerara windows and a whimsical stencil detail that softens the large wooden beams. In the ceiling, tin sheeting has been laid between the rafters and hanging stainless steel lights run in two parallel lines down the centre of the ceiling.

Below: The pool, which is not tiled, but made of plastered concrete, is designed to look as if it were a natural part of the landscape. The river boulders have had their velvety mossy surfaces helped along by daily applications of yoghurt. The poolside garden hearkens to the days of country living, and there, among the bromeliads, samaans and cassias, the homeowners enjoy dinner, the cares of city life washed away.

SAVING GRAY'S

JAMAICA

A businessman restores a termite-infested great house in Jamaica,
thereby preserving 200 years of history and giving the architects and decorator unique challenges

Adapted from original article by **Grace Cameron**   Photography by **Franz Marzouca**

Located south of Annotto Bay, St Mary (about an hour's drive from Kingston), Gray's Inn gazes out onto the sea from a hilltop perch known as Fairy Land.

Fifteen years ago, when it was bought by its current owner, a Kingston businessman who prefers to remain anonymous, the one-time sugar plantation showed little of its former glory. Built in the arts and crafts architectural style (high ceilings, open spaces) that was popular in Britain of the 1800s, the great house was termite-ridden and sagging under old age. It took 10 months just to get rid of the termites under the pine hardwood floors, and roughly four more years to transform the house into an elegant and comfortable private residence.

The story of Gray's Inns began with John Elmslie who created the estate, circa early 1800s, and named it after the Inns of Court in London, England, where barristers are trained and are called to the Bar. The estate was sold in the early 1900s to Charles Pringle, a planter, and was producing sugar up to the mid-1970s.

The great house has 17 rooms—five bedrooms and bathrooms; front entrance hall, living, dining, family rooms and a study; breakfast area, and the bedroom/office in the attic. It covers 7,909 square feet of living space—6,595 and 1,314 in the attic.

To start the restoration, the trees around the house were taken down (to get rid of the termites), and the metal storm shutters on the windows were replaced with white wooden window boxes to give the house a light and airy feel. The hardwood floors (thought to be the original) were sanded and refinished. Kingston-based architects Roy Stephenson and Associates kept the floor plan but added a front porch that flows into the family room. The back of the house (behind the dining room) was extended with a breakfast nook framed by wooden lattice work for a breezy, relaxed atmosphere.

The largely unused attic, which had been accessible only from the back through the kitchen, was given a new purpose. The architects opened up the space by cutting out a part of the living room ceiling and building a staircase leading to the upstairs. From the attic, they carved out a spacious master bedroom, bathroom and closet and added a front porch off the bedroom that takes advantage of the sweeping vista of the sea and surrounding countryside.

It took two years to decorate and furnish the great house with its high ceilings, disproportioned windows and other idiosyncrasies. Interior decorator Hester Rousseau used canvas blinds to disguise the disproportioned windows and canopies in pink, green and brown in the bedrooms to hide the small, high windows. In the dark living room, sandwiched by the rest of the house, she used large mirrors and reflected wall sconces to bring in "as much reflective light as possible". She draped the front entrance hall in an imported floral fabric because of the peeling wall plaster. In the corners of the room where the fabric could not naturally fit, she brought in an artist who hand painted the exact pattern into those crevices.

To furnish the house, Rousseau took her lead from the Victorian mood of the pieces she found there—a 14-foot dark wood dining room table with chairs, a chandelier in the formal dining room, and a piece in the entry way. Owing to the scale and position of the door between the living and dining rooms, it was necessary to find pairs of furniture, or pieces that balanced each other on opposite sides of the room.

"We would find one piece which we then had to have copied. Plus, almost everything had to be altered and that took a long time. The four-poster iron beds, for example, had to be extended to make them larger," Rousseau explained.

Today, Gray's Inn sparkles with love and attention. The housekeeper Polly Pasmore says it takes a full working day—8 a.m. to 3.30 p.m. just to polish all the brass accessories, such as the ancient brass keys, some close to six inches long; the details on just about every door; and the four-poster beds.

154

From the attic, architects carved out a spacious bedroom, bathroom and closet and added a front porch that takes advantage of the sweeping vistas of the sea and surrounding countryside. They also created a walk-in linen closet and at the back, an office/bedroom space.

It took two years to decorate Gray's Inn in the manner which it deserved. Precisely-chosen splashes of colour relieve the formality of the imposing four-poster bed and regal furniture.

Pink ottomans add an almost playful touch. Striped, informal curtains add a dash of the unexpected in what might otherwise be a too perfectly coordinated room.

Left: The living room was sandwiched by the rest of the house and made even darker by wood panelling. The decorator used mirrors to introduce more light. Plaid ottoman replies to the pink and green floral upholstery.

Below: Every detail is attended to with meticulous care. A housekeeper and other fulltime employees stick to a rigid schedule to maintain the gleam of the place. Mirror and lamp help banish darkness.

Far left: A chandelier and 14-foot dark dining table with chairs were found in the decaying house. These pieces provided the cue for the decorator who needed to stay true to the history and spirit of the house. Stripes add an almost festive air.

Left: Sideboard in dining room sparkles with highly-polished silver. The large mirror and lamps introduce much-needed light.

Far left: This large terrace lies to the front of the house and drawing room is off this area.

Left: Unlike the rest of the house, the kitchen, with its chicken-wire cupboards, is simple and rustic.

163

Far left: A peacock struts across the grounds to the back of the house. The pool area lies just beyond the steps.

Left: Once a crumbling great house, Gray's Inn beckons with the relaxed country charm that the social and political elite find alluring. The owner and his family visit some weekends and holidays. But Gray's Inn needs never feel neglected again.

THROUGH
THE DOOR

C A N O U A N

A villa on Canouan Island rejects international style and conjures up the spirit of the tropics, from Mexico to Bali to Morocco

Adapted from original article by **Elena Korach**   Photography by **Julie Webster**

This is the story of a door.

The Indian door separates the outside world from a secluded familiar space. It defines a border and invites the guest into a courtyard. Stepping across that doorway means entering a different world, where the living is easy, where understatement and friendliness are the governing rules. Here, each door hides the unexpected.

Happyland is the villa of architect and designer, Antonio Ferrari, who designed the Carenage Bay Resort on Canouan Island and decided to make the place his part-time home. He wanted to create two living units for his children, two houses clustered around the swimming pool. But the two units melt into a sequence of different shapes and spaces.

This house is all about surprise and uniqueness. No two bedrooms look alike, no two bathrooms are the same. The design is manifestly against straight lines and perfection—instead, it's pro-sensuality and texture. Always be cautious about people who are afraid to touch. Sterility is death; movement is life. Every surface here invites you to touch it, to feel it. Every wall is painted in ever-changing colours. Every door awakens your curiosity.

Throughout the house, there are echoes of tropical or Mediterranean memories: the adobe walls, textured in the colours of the sun and earth, of the sea and the sky; roofs that recall Bermuda, but also Mexico and the Greek islands. There are hand-painted Mexican tiles, cotto floors and coloured Mexican sinks.

Precious woods abound—the aquari-quari columns of the Amazonas forest, the acapu rails, the ipe windows, the teak pool chairs, the bamboo roofs.

The furnishings were collected from all over the tropics, from Mexico to Bail, Morocco to India, but also echoing Provence and Lombardy. Collectibles from the world over invite the telling of stories: a collection of Moroccan coffee cans; a vase full of oval sacred stones from the Ganges; a series of copper pots and pans hanging in the kitchen fireplace.

The staircases leading to the bedrooms wind around a tropical garden. Look up, and through a hole in the roof, and you see sky, a deep blue square against a sunny yellow ceiling. The walls, the mirror frames, the plaster bedheads were painted by the architect. The curtains and bedspreads were made in India according to Ferrari's design.

The air flows freely through louvred windows and around the cathedral-high ceilings, from the Indian stone grids in the gables of the kitchen roofs to the chimneys of the central square roofs or the living rooms.

The pool area is lit with torches in Moroccan vases. And then, there is the view, the magnificent view—of the emerald golf course and all the shades of turquoise and blue of the sea, the reef and the Caribbean sky.

No architectural statements are needed. No show off. The large spaces are to live better, not to impress. The high ceilings for the breezes, not for show.

The architect defines his home this way: "As cosy as a used slipper."

Right: The Indian door invites the guest into a courtyard. Stepping across that threshold means entering a different world, where straight lines are abhorred and imperfection adds value.

Left: In the drawing room, high ceilings are for breezes, not show. It's a sensual room that invites the hand to caress the adobe walls and texture of the wood.

Above: The dining room, off the drawing room, echoes the Mediterranean, with textured walls the colour of the sun. The air flows freely through louvred windows. The large spaces are to live better, not to impress.

In the rustic, blue and white kitchen, big, noisy dinners are the norm.

173

Below: In one of the eight bedrooms, the colours are inspired by the reefs and oceans and Caribbean sky. Curtains and bedspreads were manufactured in India according to the design of the homeowner.

Right: The seaside theme continues in the bathroom where the mirror frame was painted by the architect himself. The worn, unfinished, imperfect look throughout the villa is deliberate. The architect was inspired by the Japanese concept of wabi-sabi: use and imperfection give uniqueness and value to the object.

Left: The outdoor shower, with ochre walls and earth-toned tiles, evokes memories of Mexico. Throughout the villa, there is the influence of world cultures—Bali, Morocco, India, the Greek islands.

Above: The swimming pool area maintains the spare, rustic mood with the teak pool chairs and blue and yellow tiled table. From there, one can embrace stunning views of the Carenage Bay; the emerald green of the golf course; and all shades of turquoise and blue of the Caribbean Sea and sky.

A KNIGHT'S TALE

B A R B A D O S

An English rock star gets domestic among the heliconias at his home in Barbados

By **Neysha Soodeen**   Photography by **Bob Kiss**

Once upon a time, in a land far, far away, there lived a boy who dreamt he would grow up to be a king and live in a beautiful palace, surrounded by magnificent gardens with angelic music filling the air.

And that boy grew up, and his dreams were fulfilled. He was knighted and his palace, located in Barbados and spectacularly appointed, is surrounded by tropical foliage. The music filling the air is his own.

Sir Cliff Richard, the beloved English rock star of the Seventies, fell in love with the island of Barbados in the Nineties when he visited his friend David Lloyd, who was at the time, developing an area of land, called Sugar Hill, on the west coast of the island. Enchanted by the spectacular views, Sir Cliff bought the land and started to design his house with the help of architect David Spinks. He knew exactly what he wanted, and within two years, the house was complete.

"The house was designed specifically for entertaining" Sir Cliff said. "I wanted the entire house open to the view, and to the gardens." Sir Cliff has an almost fatherly love for his garden. The pruning does not stop for the conversation. He talks with a pair of clippers in his hand, while roaming from the heliconias to the ginger lilies.

Coral Sundown is unique, something of a paradox. Although recently built, the house has the presence of an older and more venerable building. Although everything has its place, the house does not feel overly formal or pretentious but welcoming. Built over a gully is the bridge leading the way to the main entrance of Coral Sundown. Once though the doors, visitors can't miss the spectacular view of cane fields and the vibrant blue of the Caribbean Sea.

The formal living room, which is the first room guests enter, is divided into four small seating areas, filled with artwork from across the globe and vases of freshly-cut flowers from Sir Cliff's garden. The main entertaining area, however, seems to be the large covered patio with comfortable rattan furniture bought in Barbados. Music from his latest album is piped though the entire house, without the obstructions of bulky speakers, but seems to come out of nowhere.

Adjacent to the patio is the dining room with its colossal chandelier. When Sir Cliff first had the chandelier made by John Burgess, he wanted to hide the main support. Burgess did this by concocting a wild maze of wrought iron, which distracts from the main stay, and forms the focal point of the room.

And where does this king sleep? In a boudoir with an enormous Egyptian painting hanging directly above his bed. "This painting was a present to me. I was invited to a charity function in Germany, which I attended. The theme was Egyptian, and this painting had captured my attention. I had asked the organiser of the event if it were possible to buy it, but he said No!" Sir Cliff said, with a smirk. "The painting was wrapped and sent to me as a present. I was very surprised and very grateful."

But perhaps the most wonderful part of this palace is the king's bathing area. "I wanted this room to feel as if it were part of the outdoors. So I had this beautiful trompe l'oeil painted by Linda Roach on the walls. My favourite part is the monkey with the watering can by the shower!"

Right: Sir Cliff Richard spends quality time tending to his garden. The constant, soothing sound of water trickling into the pond is heard from the adjacent dining room.

Left: Rattan furniture in the patio provides a comfortable and chic retreat, which blends naturally with the bountiful garden.

Below: The homeowner might be a famous English rock star but his living room, which melts into the covered patio, is a showpiece of stately charm.

Right: This corner forms part of the living room, the unusual wrought-iron base of the glass table and swirling lamp contrast with the more venerable-looking pieces.

Far right: The dining room is open to the garden and pool area. The wrought-iron chandelier, which resembles a tangle of jungle vines, was designed by John Burgess.

Right: The huge Egyptian painting was a gift and inspired the mood for the master bedroom.

Below: Even in his bathroom, the rock star could not bear to be away from the glorious outdoors, so artist Linda Roach painted a trompe l'oeil on the walls.